Original title:
The Art of Healing

Copyright © 2024 Swan Charm
All rights reserved.

Author: Paula Raudsepp
ISBN HARDBACK: 978-9916-79-033-5
ISBN PAPERBACK: 978-9916-79-034-2
ISBN EBOOK: 978-9916-79-035-9

Divergent Pathways to Peace

In the quiet woods we tread,
Footsteps soft on ancient trails.
Paths diverge beneath the trees,
Whispers of the wind unveil.

One leads to a sunlit glade,
Where laughter dances in the breeze.
The other, shrouded in cool shade,
Offers solace, hearts at ease.

Every choice a tender thread,
Woven in the fabric bright.
Seeking peace where hope is spread,
Guided by the stars at night.

Murmurs of Resurgence

In the depths of winter's grasp,
New life stirs beneath the frost.
Silent murmurs slowly rasp,
Echoes of what seemed long lost.

Tender shoots through soil rise high,
Making their way toward the sun.
Life's resilience will not die,
From shadows, new beginnings run.

Buds awaken, blooms ignite,
Colors bursting into view.
In the struggle, pure delight,
Nature's song rings ever true.

Healing in the Reflection

In the mirror of the soul,
Truths reveal their gentle face.
Every flaw, a vital role,
In the journey toward grace.

Ripples dance upon the stream,
Carrying whispers of the past.
In still waters, dreams redeem,
Finding strength in shadows cast.

With each glance, we heal and grow,
Learning from the scars we bear.
Embrace the ebb, embrace the flow,
In every heartbeat, show we care.

Symphony of Wellness

Notes of life compose the air,
Harmony within the mind.
Every breath, a sweet affair,
The rhythm that we seek to find.

In laughter's echo, joy abounds,
Strumming strings of hope and light.
Connections weave in tender rounds,
Crafting melodies so bright.

Together, we can sing the song,
A chorus rich with lives entwined.
In this symphony, we belong,
Healing hearts and freeing minds.

Illuminated Journey

In the soft glow of dawn,
Shadows dance on the ground.
Steps taken with purpose,
The world calls, profound.

Pathways lined with gold,
Every turn whispers fate.
Mountains loom in the distance,
Adventure won't wait.

Clouds drift in the sky,
Echoes of dreams soar high.
With heart wide open,
Beneath the vast, blue sky.

Stars guide the wayfarers,
Through valleys deep and wide.
In the light of the moon,
Hope is our faithful guide.

With lessons on this road,
And memories that last,
Each moment illuminated,
A journey unsurpassed.

The Wind's Gentle Touch

Through leaves the whispers play,
A symphony in green.
The wind finds tender ways,
In nature's serene scene.

Caressing fields of wheat,
With every breath, it flows.
A soft and sweet retreat,
Beneath the skies that glow.

Dancing through the trees,
In a waltz of delight,
The wind sings to the seas,
As day turns into night.

Carrying dreams afar,
It swirls with grace and might.
Guiding the wandering star,
In the embrace of night.

So let the breezes speak,
Of stories yet untold.
In each gentle caress,
Find warmth when days feel cold.

Serendipitous Landscapes

Wander through the unknown,
Where colors blend and play.
In every hidden stone,
Life finds a charming way.

Mountains kiss the sky,
While rivers sing with glee.
In this grand, vast canvas,
Nature invites us to see.

Fields awash with blooms,
Each petal a soft sigh.
In sunlight's warm embrace,
Hearts learn to fly high.

Unexpected paths reveal,
The beauty in the bold.
In moments pure, we feel,
The treasures we hold.

With every step we take,
A dance unfolds anew.
In landscapes full of grace,
Our spirits find their view.

Finding Grace in Loss

In the echoes of goodbye,
Memories softly fade.
Yet in the heart they lie,
A love that won't evade.

Through shadows we may tread,
With tears that gently flow.
Each step can be a thread,
Weaving strength from sorrow.

In emptiness we find,
A quiet, shining peace.
From heartache's tangled bind,
Comes a chance for release.

The beauty of a smile,
Can bloom through darkest nights.
In loss, we'll walk a mile,
Towards new, hopeful heights.

For every end we face,
A new beginning gleams.
In finding grace in loss,
We carry on our dreams.

Resurgence of the Silent

Whispers rise from shadows deep,
Voices lost, now dare to speak.
A spark ignites, a flame renews,
In silence blooms, a world anew.

Hands once bound, now grasp the light,
Breaking free from endless night.
In quiet strength, the heart returns,
With every pulse, the spirit yearns.

Echoes of the past take flight,
Songs unsung break into sight.
A symphony of hope unfolds,
In every heart, a dream retold.

From ashes rise the brave and bold,
With stories rich, their truth unfolds.
In gentle courage, they reclaim,
The courage found within their name.

Resurgence whispers through the air,
Silent strength begins to share.
In every heart, a flame ignites,
Resurgence blooms in starry nights.

Labyrinth of Emotions

Winding paths of heart's delight,
Twisting shadows, chasing light.
Every turn, a truth revealed,
In this maze, our fate is sealed.

Joy and sorrow dance entwined,
Echoes of the past remind.
Laughter mingles with the tears,
In labyrinths, we face our fears.

Threads of longing weave the way,
Hints of love in disarray.
Finding peace amidst the strife,
Guided by the pulse of life.

Mirrors reflect each hidden part,
Every corner holds a heart.
In this puzzle, we explore,
Unraveling what lies in store.

Though uncertain, keep the pace,
Every step, a new embrace.
Through the maze, we find our home,
In the heart, we freely roam.

Tidal Waves of Change

Crashing waves, relentless tide,
Rising currents, dreams collide.
Each new dawn brings shifting sands,
Change is here, with open hands.

Whispers of the ocean's roar,
In every wave, a chance for more.
Tempests rage, yet softly fade,
In transformation, fears invade.

Colors blend in sunset's grace,
As shadows dance in twilight's space.
With every push, the heart must grow,
Tidal waves will ebb and flow.

In the storm, resilience found,
Waves of change shall know no bound.
Ride the crest, embrace the fall,
In the chaos, hear the call.

Life will shift like sea and sky,
Through the storms, we learn to fly.
With every wave, the soul expands,
Tidal forces shape our hands.

Unfurling the Dreams

Petals open to the sun,
Whispers soft, the day's begun.
In each heart, a dream takes flight,
Unfolding truths in morning light.

A canvas bright with wishes made,
Brush of hope and fears displayed.
Every color tells a tale,
In dreams we rise, we will not fail.

From the depths, the voice of one,
Yearning for the battles won.
With every step, the future gleams,
As we weave the threads of dreams.

Paths uncharted lie ahead,
In the silence, courage bred.
Unfurling gently, take your stand,
With open heart, embrace the land.

In the dance of fate and chance,
Life invites us to advance.
Together, let our spirits soar,
Unfurling dreams forevermore.

Raindrops on the Spirit

Soft whispers fall from gray,
Each droplet sings a song,
They touch the heart gently,
Reviving hope all day.

In puddles, dreams are mirrored,
Reflections of the past,
Every splash a memory,
In the silence, they've stirred.

Sweet aromas rise and dance,
As fragrances unite,
Nature's balm, a pure embrace,
In rain's soft, tender glance.

Clouds drift, a soothing veil,
Covering the weary mind,
Through each tear of joy, we sail,
In this world, love we find.

Healing Hands

In gentle touch, a spark ignites,
A warmth like summer sun,
Each hand extends a lifeline,
Easing pain till it takes flight.

With every press, the heart unfolds,
Revealing whispers deep,
A symphony of strength and care,
In silence, magic holds.

The world softens in their grace,
A dance of hope and trust,
In fragile hands, we find our place,
A bond that's pure and just.

These hands weave love into the night,
Mending souls with ease,
With a light that feels so right,
Transforming fear to flight.

Mosaic of Moments

Fragments of time, a scattered song,
Each piece tells a tale,
Colors clash in beauty's throng,
In chaos, we belong.

A whispered laugh beneath the stars,
Echoes in the breeze,
With every scar, we bear our scars,
Creating memories.

Joy interwoven with the ache,
Threads of light and shade,
In life's vast tapestry we make,
All the moments laid.

We stitch them close with fragile hands,
Each pattern tells its part,
Together, we create like bands,
A mosaic from the heart.

Breathing Space

In the stillness, find a breath,
Each inhale, a gift of grace,
Exhaling whispers of the past,
Inviting peace, a sweet bequest.

Where thoughts drift like dandelion seeds,
Floating softly in the air,
A moment's pause is what we need,
To feel the love that's everywhere.

With every heartbeat, take it slow,
Ease the rush of endless days,
In this quiet, let life flow,
A dance within the space we sow.

The world recedes, just you and me,
A canvas clear and bright,
In breathing space, we're truly free,
Embracing love and light.

Unfolding the Heart

In whispers soft, the heart unveils,
Layers of love, where truth prevails.
Tender moments, fragile and bright,
Guiding us through the silent night.

Each beat a story, a breath of grace,
Carving the paths, we dare to chase.
Fears dissolve in the warm embrace,
Unfolding light in the shaded space.

With every tear, a seed is sown,
In the soil of pain, where dreams are grown.
Opening wide, the heart expands,
Offering kindness through open hands.

Together we dance, in ebb and flow,
In the garden of trust, love's blossoms grow.
A journey shared, two souls ignite,
Unfolding the heart, we take flight.

Wounds Turned to Wisdom

In silence kept, the wounds will speak,
Lessons hidden in scars so deep.
Time weaves tales of sorrow's thread,
Transforming pain to wisdom spread.

A gentle sigh, as seasons shift,
Gifts of struggle, the heart does lift.
From ashes rise, a brighter view,
Wounds turned to wisdom, a life anew.

The echoes linger, but hearts are strong,
In the dance of healing, we belong.
Finding peace where shadows lay,
Wounds turn golden with each new day.

With courage born from deep despair,
We learn to breathe in lighter air.
Our battles faced, our stories blend,
Wounds turned to wisdom, they transcend.

Chasing the Dawn

Awake in dreams where shadows flee,
Chasing the dawn, we seek to be free.
Colors ignite in the morning light,
Whispers of hope, the day takes flight.

With every step, the world anew,
Sunrise blooms in radiant hue.
Embracing change, we dance along,
Chasing the dawn, where we belong.

Moments of magic in gleams of gold,
Stories of wonder, waiting to be told.
Hands held tight, together we run,
Chasing the dawn, two hearts as one.

Let shadows linger, we won't relent,
In the warmth of light, our fears are spent.
With every heartbeat, we rise and yawn,
Chasing the dawn until the night is gone.

Echoes of Resilience

In the stillness, echoes sound,
Whispers of strength in battles found.
Bearing storms that shook the ground,
Resilience blooms, where hope is crowned.

Through darkest nights, we find our way,
Stars will guide us, come what may.
In every heartbeat, stories collide,
Echoes of resilience, our fierce pride.

With open hearts, we stand our ground,
Turning the pain into beauty profound.
Each step forward, a step that's true,
Echoes of resilience, strong and new.

Together we rise, united and bold,
In the face of the storms, our spirits hold.
With every challenge, we learn, we grow,
Echoes of resilience, forever they flow.

Unfolding Peace

In gentle whispers, hope will bloom,
As dawn awakens, chasing gloom.
With every breath, the heart will mend,
A quiet journey never ends.

Through fields of dreams where silence sighs,
The soul finds solace, light in skies.
With open arms, the world stands still,
In tender moments, peace can fill.

Each step a dance, a sacred grace,
In every corner, love's embrace.
The past will fade, the future gleams,
Awash in sunlight, hope redeems.

Beneath the stars, we gather close,
In shared reflections, hearts engross.
As time unfolds, we learn to see,
The beauty found in harmony.

So let us wander, hand in hand,
Embracing change, we understand.
A journey long, yet ever sweet,
In every heartbeat, peace we meet.

Layers of Recovery

In shadows cast, the truth appears,
Each layer peels to confront fears.
A tapestry of scars and grace,
In tender light, we find our place.

With every tear, a seed is sown,
In fertile ground, growth is known.
The heart, once heavy, starts to rise,
Through storms we learn to realize.

Quiet moments, deep and still,
Can heal the wounds we never will.
Each whisper shared, a bond unites,
In fragile strength, we find our rights.

The journey's path is never straight,
With every turn, we navigate.
Yet through the trials, we reclaim,
The essence of our heartfelt flame.

So let the layers slowly peel,
In truth and love, we start to heal.
Each story told is part of growth,
In shared connection, we find hope.

Gifts of the Broken

In shards of light, the fractured show,
Beauty lingers where hurt can grow.
Each piece reflects a sacred chance,
In brokenness, we find our dance.

Through jagged edges, stories flow,
A tapestry of real and slow.
With open hearts, we mend the seams,
What once was lost becomes our dreams.

In every crack, a lesson waits,
To see the world through honest states.
Compassion blooms where pain has kissed,
In shared experience, we exist.

The gifts we hold from trials faced,
Are treasures wrapped in dreams embraced.
Together strong, we rise anew,
From brokenness, our hearts break through.

So cherish all that life would give,
In wounds and wonders, we shall live.
In every heart, a truth unspoken,
The strength of love in gifts unbroken.

Gentle Unraveling

Petals fall in quiet grace,
Whispers of a soft embrace.
Threads of time begin to fray,
In this dance of night and day.

Stars above begin to weep,
Secrets that the shadows keep.
Gentle hands will pull apart,
Unraveling the woven heart.

The moonlight glimmers on the stream,
Nature's breath, a soothing dream.
Crickets sing a lullaby,
As the world begins to sigh.

Daylight fades, colors unwind,
In the silence, peace we find.
With each moment, layers shed,
In the calm, where fears are fed.

Autumn winds will softly call,
As the leaves begin to fall.
Every ending breathes a start,
In the gentle, unraveling art.

Rebirth in Silence

In the hush, a seed will grow,
Where the quiet rivers flow.
Dormant dreams awaken now,
To the whispers of a vow.

Beneath the frost, a spark ignites,
Casting warmth on winter nights.
In the silence, life returns,
As the flame of hope still burns.

Breaking through the frozen ground,
Beauty lies in what is found.
Each new leaf a promise made,
In the stillness, fears do fade.

Glimmers of a vibrant hue,
Colors brightening the view.
With each breath, a chance to feel,
Rebirth speaks, a spirit real.

In the shadows, light will seep,
As the world begins to leap.
Through the silence, hearts will sing,
In rebirth, we're offering.

Portraits of Hope

Canvas stretched, colors collide,
Stories bound in every stride.
Brushstrokes tell a tale anew,
In the heart, a vibrant view.

Laughter dances on the page,
Each emotion, raw and sage.
Shadows cast by dreams once feared,
Now the light, it's bright and cleared.

Every tear is made of light,
Painting paths through darkest night.
In the hues, we find our way,
Chasing clouds to brighter day.

Whispers weave through gentle hands,
Creating worlds, diverse lands.
In each frame, a voice will rise,
Lifted by the painted skies.

Hope, a portrait in the dawn,
Every brush brings forth the song.
With each scene that unfolds clear,
A masterpiece of love and cheer.

Unchained Melody

In the night, a song escapes,
Carried through the dusk and shapes.
Each note dances on the breeze,
As the heart begins to seize.

Whispers echo in the dark,
Strumming strings, igniting spark.
Footsteps light the path we tread,
Together, where the music led.

Every silence filled with sound,
In this love, our souls are bound.
With a rhythm, wild and free,
Unchained melody takes thee.

From the shadows, bright and bold,
Stories of our dreams retold.
In the harmony, we find,
A symphony of heart and mind.

As the dawn begins to break,
Every fear we gently shake.
In the cadence, hearts ignite,
Unchained melody, pure light.

Bridges Beyond Pain

In shadows deep, we learn to tread,
Across the chasms, where hopes once bled.
With every step, we mend the fray,
Building bridges along the way.

Through storms we sail, through trials we grow,
With hands united, we start to know.
The path may twist, but hearts remain,
Together we rise, transcending pain.

In whispered dreams, we find our light,
The dawn breaks clear, dispelling night.
Each scar a tale, each laugh a song,
Turning the weak into the strong.

A journey forged in love and trust,
In every stumble, we find we must.
Look beyond, there lies the dawn,
Where bridges built lead to the lawn.

With open hearts, we take the chance,
To dance in joy, to laugh, to prance.
On bridges made of love and grace,
We find our strength, our sacred space.

Flames of Forgiveness

In embers glows a tender spark,
A flicker bright, igniting dark.
With every breath, the past we free,
As flames of trust bend toward the sea.

The hurt dismissed, the weight laid down,
Each flick openly wears a crown.
From ashes rise the new terrain,
Where empathy's fire will remain.

Forgiveness flows like rivers clear,
Washing away all doubt and fear.
In tender hands, we fan the flames,
Rekindling love that softly claims.

Mark each step on this glowing path,
Leave behind the shadows' wrath.
With warmth we wrap the wounded heart,
And pledge to never drift apart.

Together we rise, like phoenix bright,
From charred remains towards the light.
In flames of hope, our spirits soar,
In each embrace, we heal once more.

Cultivating Wholeness

In gardens where the wildflowers dance,
We plant the seeds of love's expanse.
With every drop of hope we sow,
In the soil of trust, our spirits grow.

Nurtured by the morning light,
Each tender shoot, a wondrous sight.
Through storms that come, resilient we stand,
Together growing, hand in hand.

Weaving dreams with threads of grace,
In wholeness found, we embrace space.
Where broken paths lead to vast skies,
A tapestry of life that never lies.

In every crack, the beauty shines,
The healing journey, love defines.
Cultivating joy, amidst the pain,
Together, we dance in the rain.

With open hearts and minds as one,
In life's embrace, we've just begun.
From seeds of hope, our lives unfold,
In harmony, our stories told.

Veils of Vulnerability

Beneath the veil, our truths reside,
In soft whispers, we cannot hide.
With every tear, a veil unspun,
Revealing warmth, where love's begun.

In gentle touch, we find our way,
With fragile hearts, we choose to stay.
Each layer peeled, a step toward peace,
Among the fears, we find release.

In vulnerability, we learn to trust,
Embracing all, it's truly just.
Our stories shared in quiet grace,
In every smile, we find our place.

Unveil the masks, let spirits soar,
In raw connections, we explore.
With hearts exposed, we find our might,
As true reflections become our light.

So let us stand, unguarded, free,
In the tapestry of you and me.
Through veils of doubt, a bond is spun,
In vulnerability, love's never done.

Roots of Rejuvenation

In the earth, we find our peace,
Nurtured by time, our worries cease.
Each season whispers tales of old,
In roots so deep, our dreams unfold.

Nature's breath, a calming sigh,
Beneath the branches, we will lie.
With every leaf, a story told,
In whispers soft, our hearts be bold.

From shadows past, new life will rise,
Sunlight dances, brightens skies.
In harmony, we learn to thrive,
With every heartbeat, we survive.

In unity, the earth we tread,
Through tangled paths, our spirits spread.
With every bloom, a promise true,
The roots of life, we turn anew.

Embrace the cycle, let it flow,
Through joy and sorrow, we will grow.
In every season, love's refrain,
The roots of us, a sweet domain.

Serenade of the Senses

A fragrance swirls upon the breeze,
Carried softly, like gentle pleas.
Colors dance in radiant light,
Awakening the heart's delight.

The taste of honey, sweet and pure,
A simple joy that we adore.
With every sound, the world sings clear,
In harmony, we gather near.

Textures weave a soothing spell,
In touch, we find the stories tell.
The rush of waves upon the shore,
An endless rhythm, we explore.

With open eyes, we seek to find,
The beauty in the ties that bind.
A symphony of life unfolds,
Each moment precious, as it molds.

Connect the dots with every breath,
In life's embrace, we conquer death.
In sensory delight, we see,
The serenade of you and me.

Journey to Center

With every step, the path unwinds,
In solitude, our truth we find.
A silent quest, where shadows dwell,
In deep reflection, we compel.

The river's flow, a guiding song,
In stillness, we know we belong.
The heart beats steady, strong and clear,
In sacred space, we shed our fear.

The mountains tall, they call our name,
A journey inward, never the same.
Each turn reveals a glimpse of light,
As stars awaken through the night.

In whispered thoughts, we plant the seed,
Finding strength in every need.
The circle turns, our spirits rise,
In every moment, wisdom lies.

To center is to learn and grow,
To nurture all that we can know.
In this journey, pure and free,
We discover who we're meant to be.

Colors of Kindness

A gentle smile, a warming light,
In simple acts, our hearts take flight.
With open hands, we share our grace,
The colors bloom in every place.

In laughter shared, the world feels bright,
With kindness woven, day and night.
A touch, a word—so pure, refined,
In every heart, our souls aligned.

Through trials faced, together we stand,
In unity, we lend a hand.
The canvas spreads, with hues anew,
In shades of love, we paint our view.

From whispered hopes to big embrace,
The colors blend, no need for space.
With every deed, the kindness thrives,
In vibrant strokes, our spirit strives.

So let us color all we see,
In kindness rich, we'll always be.
The rainbow flows from me to you,
In every bond, a love so true.

Hands of Compassion

In a world that's often cold,
Reach out with warmth untold.
A gentle touch can heal the pain,
Bringing hope like steady rain.

With open hearts, we lend our grace,
Finding love in every place.
Together, we can make a stand,
With caring hearts and steady hand.

In silence, kindness speaks so loud,
A tender heart, a faithful crowd.
Through storms of life, together brave,
We become the light we crave.

In every act of selfless care,
We weave a bond that's ever rare.
The hands of compassion never tire,
They lift us up, ignite our fire.

So let us plant this seed of peace,
In every soul, may kindness increase.
For when we love and when we share,
The world becomes a brighter air.

Mapping the Heart's Terrain

In the depths where feelings grow,
Lies a map that we must know.
Through valleys low and mountains high,
Our hearts navigate, reaching the sky.

With every thrum, a path revealed,
Secrets of the heart unsealed.
Connections formed with every beat,
Guiding souls, making us complete.

From joy to sorrow, love to grief,
Each experience brings belief.
As we trace our journeys wide,
We create a map, our hearts abide.

With gentle hands, we sketch the lines,
Through solitude and shared designs.
The heart's terrain, a sacred ground,
Where every voice can be profound.

In this landscape of human ties,
Compassion flows, and hope complies.
Together we explore the vast,
Mapping the moments that we've cast.

Reimagining Tomorrow

In dreams we craft a brighter view,
A world where hope feels fresh and new.
With every thought, we help to build,
A future where our hearts are filled.

We sketch the sky with colors bold,
A canvas where the dreams unfold.
With every step, we break the mold,
Creating stories waiting to be told.

In unity, we'll find our way,
Together, shaping a better day.
Through trials faced, we learn to soar,
Reimagining what lies in store.

With hearts on fire, we'll rise and stand,
Building bridges across the land.
A tapestry of hope and grace,
In every smile, we find our place.

So let us dream, and let us dare,
Together, we're creating where.
With open minds and loving hearts,
Reimagining tomorrow starts.

Silent Spring

In whispers soft, the earth awakes,
As nature stirs, the silence breaks.
With gentle hues of green and gold,
A story of rebirth unfolds.

Beneath the frost, the flowers sleep,
While tender roots in silence weep.
But soon the sun will warm the ground,
As life returns, all joys abound.

The robin sings a sweet refrain,
Soft echoes of the springtime rain.
With every drop, a promise made,
In silent spring, our fears do fade.

As blossoms bloom, the world awakes,
Creating paths where love partakes.
In harmony, the earth will sing,
A hymn of life that spring will bring.

So let us cherish this gentle time,
In nature's arms, we find our rhyme.
For in the quiet, beauty lies,
A silent spring, where hope will rise.

Lanterns in the Dark

In shadows deep, we find our way,
With lanterns bright, we chase the gray.
Each flicker whispers, secrets kept,
In whispered dreams, our hopes are slept.

The night holds fears, but light will guide,
Through tangled paths, we'll walk with pride.
With every step, the darkness fades,
As lanterns shine, the light cascades.

Stars above, like lanterns glow,
In the stillness, their soft flow.
We count the wonders, one by one,
With every breath, our journey's begun.

Together we will weave the light,
And banish shadows, take to flight.
For in our hearts, the fires spark,
Guiding souls, through lanterns in the dark.

So hold your lantern, shine it bright,
Let love be your eternal light.
And when the dark seems all around,
Remember, in hope, our hearts are bound.

The Quiet Restoration

In silence deep, we gather rain,
Each droplet falls, to heal the pain.
A gentle breeze, the trees embrace,
Restoring peace, with nature's grace.

The brook hums softly, tunes of old,
In whispered notes, new stories told.
With every pause, we breathe anew,
In quiet moments, life feels true.

The sun peeks in, through leafy green,
A golden touch, on spaces unseen.
We seek the calm, in twilight's glow,
Restoration comes, like seeds we sow.

Paths of stillness, hold our fears,
In quietude, we shed our tears.
Together we mend what life has torn,
In quiet restoration, we are reborn.

Let's find the peace within our hearts,
In every stillness, beauty starts.
The quiet call of soul's refrain,
Restoring joy, where hope remains.

Harvest of the Heart

In fields of gold, our dreams take flight,
With every seed, we plant the light.
The sun will shine, the rains will fall,
In harvest time, we'll reap it all.

With hands we toil, beneath blue skies,
The fruits of love, in laughter rise.
Each grain the earth gives us to share,
A testament to the hope we bear.

The bounty calls, and we must heed,
Together strong, in every deed.
In gratitude, our hearts expand,
As we embrace what life has planned.

Through seasons passed, and years that flow,
We've learned to nurture, let love grow.
In every morsel, joy imparts,
In this great harvest, the song of hearts.

So let us gather, hand in hand,
In unity, across this land.
For every heartbeat plays its part,
In the cherished harvest of the heart.

Fusion of Dreams

When night descends, our visions gleam,
In tapestry woven, the threads of dream.
Each whisper dances, a soft embrace,
In the fusion of dreams, we find our place.

With open minds, we share the skies,
Two souls entwined, where passion lies.
Through starlit paths, we weave together,
In every moment, we chase forever.

A melody sweet, in silence flows,
The language of love, only we know.
In every heartbeat, a rhythm starts,
In the fusion of dreams, we blend our hearts.

So take my hand, let's rise and soar,
Through realms unknown, we'll seek for more.
In every color, we craft our view,
A vibrant world, born anew.

In dreams we trust, in love we lead,
Together we bloom, as one we succeed.
For in this union, joy indeed,
In the fusion of dreams, our spirits freed.

Threads of Resilience

In storms we weave our story,
Each thread a mark of glory.
Through trials, hearts entwine,
Strength emerges, bold and fine.

With every tear, a lesson learned,
A flickering flame, the fire burned.
We stand to face the darkest night,
Guided by the spark of light.

Each thread, a whisper of the past,
In unity, we hold steadfast.
Through pain, we forge a brighter way,
A tapestry of hope in sway.

From breaking points, we gather round,
In shared belief, our strength is found.
Together, we'll face the unknown,
With threads of love, we have grown.

Resilience blooms in every heart,
A symphony of courage, we start.
In every loop, a story told,
Threads connecting, brave and bold.

The Canvas of Recovery

On canvas stretched beneath the sun,
A palette waits, our battles won.
Each brushstroke tells a tale so bright,
Of healing hearts that take to flight.

Colors splash, emotions flow,
In every hue, our spirits glow.
From ashes rise a vibrant scene,
A work of art, alive, serene.

Mistakes become the shadows cast,
With every stroke, we mend the past.
Like winter blooms in spring's embrace,
A newfound strength begins its chase.

Layers deep, our stories blend,
In every corner, hope will mend.
A masterpiece of love evokes,
Renewal whispers, gently strokes.

With every turn, the brush will glide,
In recovery, we take our stride.
The canvas waits for us anew,
To paint our dreams in shades of blue.

Breathing Life Back

In silence deep, a breath we take,
To find the strength, to mend, awake.
With whispered hopes and dreams in sight,
We spark the dawn, embrace the light.

In every heartbeat, life returns,
From shadowed past, the spirit yearns.
Through gentle winds, our voices rise,
A song of healing fills the skies.

Each step we take, a dance of grace,
In every tear, we find our place.
With courage small, yet fierce and true,
Breathing life back, we break anew.

From ashes cold, a fire grows,
In warmth, our essence freely flows.
With open arms, we greet the day,
Breathing life back, we find our way.

In every pause, the world stands still,
Awakening echoes, hearts to fill.
Together we rise, our spirits sing,
Breathing life back, love is the flame.

Echoes of Restoration

In quiet corners of the mind,
Echoes of past we seek to find.
Each memory a whisper, soft and low,
In restoration, we learn to grow.

Through shattered pieces, beauty blooms,
In silent rooms, once filled with gloom.
With open hearts, we find the grace,
To heal the scars time can't erase.

The echoes call, a soothing song,
Reminding us where we belong.
With every note, we rise again,
In tides of change, we cleanse the pain.

From echoes deep, the truth unveils,
In every struggle, love prevails.
We build anew from what was lost,
In restoration, we count the cost.

Together, we chase the evening's light,
Each echo guiding through the night.
In harmony, our hearts will soar,
Echoes of restoration, forevermore.

Alchemy of the Heart

In shadows cast by silent dreams,
Love brews beneath the seams.
Whispers of forgotten lore,
Turn to gold forevermore.

Each fleeting glance, a spark ignites,
Transforming doubt into delights.
From ashes rise, our souls entwined,
In love's embrace, all fears resigned.

The potion stirs with tender care,
Forging bonds beyond compare.
With every touch, a magic blend,
An alchemy that has no end.

Through trials faced, we find our way,
Hand in hand, come what may.
Hearts aflame, a fusion bright,
Illuminating darkest night.

In whispered vows, the truth reveals,
A tapestry of shared ideals.
In this dance, our fates align,
Crafting love, a drink divine.

Mending Through Time

Fragments of a weary past,
In time's embrace, we hold them fast.
Each scar a tale, each tear a thread,
Stitched with hope, where love's not dead.

The clock ticks soft, in gentle grace,
Repairing hearts at its own pace.
Through seasons worn, and storms we face,
We find our truth in a warm embrace.

In quiet moments, wisdom speaks,
Healing found in tender weeks.
With every sunrise, shadows fade,
Rebuilding dreams that love has made.

We gather strength from every fall,
No longer shackled by the wall.
In unity, our spirits soar,
Mending hearts forevermore.

With every heartbeat, time will weave,
A tapestry of those who believe.
In laughter shared and tears refined,
Together still, our love defined.

Spirit's Palette

An artist's brush upon the soul,
Colors blend and make us whole.
With every stroke, new worlds arise,
Painting dreams beneath the skies.

From subtle hues of dusk and dawn,
To vibrant shades where hopes are drawn.
In every line, our stories told,
A canvas rich with life unfolds.

The whispers of the heart create,
A melody that can't abate.
With passion's spark and mind's fierce flame,
We capture joy, we chase the same.

Each color sings a different song,
In unity, we find where we belong.
As spirits dance on this great stage,
Together we embrace each page.

In shadows cast by doubt and fear,
The palette brightens, visions clear.
With every blend, our souls unite,
Creating beauty, pure delight.

Embrace the Light Within

In the stillness, find your glow,
A radiant warmth that starts to flow.
Though storms may rage and shadows creep,
The light resides, your heart to keep.

In every challenge, seek the bright,
A flame that burns within your sight.
With every breath, let courage rise,
Your spirit shines like endless skies.

Through darkest valleys, pathways bend,
Embrace the light, your truest friend.
Illuminate the world you see,
With kindness shared, set your heart free.

Let love be the beacon that guides your way,
In every moment, in each day.
With open arms, and heart anew,
Embrace the light that's always true.

In whispers soft and laughter clear,
Let joy resound, let go of fear.
For in the depths of all you seek,
The light within will always speak.

Whispers of Renewal

In the quiet of the dawn,
New hopes softly stir,
Nature's breath begins anew,
Awakening the slumber.

Shadows fade with morning light,
Promises of brighter days,
Every leaf and petal sings,
In the warmth of sun's rays.

Gentle breezes sweep the earth,
Carrying dreams on their wings,
Whispers dance through the trees,
In harmony, nature sings.

With each drop of morning dew,
A fresh start is revealed,
Life unfolds in quiet grace,
A promise gently sealed.

In the heart, the spark ignites,
Of journeys fresh and true,
Embracing change, we renew,
With each dawn, life breaks through.

Threads of Resilience

In the tapestry of life,
Threads woven with care,
Each struggle shapes the pattern,
A testament laid bare.

Through the storms that test our will,
We find strength in each strand,
Colorful memories intertwined,
A fabric sturdy and grand.

Stitches of courage weave the tale,
Of battles fought and won,
With every tear that marks the cloth,
A legacy begun.

Holding tight through darkest nights,
The loom of hope stays bright,
Each moment, every heartbeat,
Threads of joy take flight.

In this quilt of shared stories,
Resilience binds us strong,
Together we are woven,
In life's beautiful song.

Embracing the Storm

Clouds gather in the sky,
A rumble shakes the ground,
Lightning dances like wild fire,
Nature's voice resound.

In the heart of chaos,
We find a strange delight,
Each drop a fierce reminder,
Of courage in the fight.

With open arms, we greet the rain,
Letting go of fear,
In the tempest's wild embrace,
We find strength to persevere.

Winds of change may howl and roar,
But we stand firm and tall,
With every gust, we toughen up,
Refusing to let fall.

After the storm has passed us by,
A clearer sky appears,
In the stillness, we discover,
The beauty born from tears.

From Ashes to Blossoms

In the wake of fiery trials,
Life finds a way to bloom,
From the ashes of despair,
Hope rises, casting gloom.

With roots deep in charred remains,
New petals push for light,
A testament to resilience,
In the hush of night.

Colors burst from barren ground,
Life's tenacious delight,
Every blossom tells a tale,
Of shadows kissed by light.

Through the darkness, strength ignites,
Each thorn a lesson learned,
From pain, beauty emerges,
In hearts that once were burned.

Embracing change, we rise anew,
With every breath, we grow,
From ashes, we find our purpose,
In the cycle of flow.

The Garden of Renewal

In shadows deep, the seedlings rise,
With every dawn, a bold reprise.
The colors blend, a vibrant sway,
As nature wakes from night to day.

Upon the leaves, the dew does gleam,
A fragrant air, a joyous dream.
Within the soil, old roots embrace,
A dance of life in sacred space.

The whispers of the winds do call,
Inviting hearts to break the fall.
With every bloom, the past releases,
In every petal, hope increases.

The sun's warm glow, a gentle guide,
Through tangled paths, we walk with pride.
In this haven, time stands still,
As dreams take flight, and spirits thrill.

And when the storms may come to play,
The garden's strength will find a way.
In every trial, the roots go deep,
A promise formed, a bond to keep.

Voices of the Unheard

In quiet corners, shadows dwell,
Untold stories yearn to swell.
A gentle sigh, a whispered prayer,
The weight of silence fills the air.

Each untold tale, a heavy weight,
In hidden hearts, they navigate.
With every breath, a truth ignites,
A chorus formed in darkened nights.

From streets of loss to mountains tall,
The echoes rise, they break the fall.
A tapestry of cries combined,
In unity, their strength aligned.

Let voices rise, let silence break,
For every heart must share its ache.
In harmony, the unheard sing,
A world reborn, their joy takes wing.

And in the light, the truth shall shine,
Together, hearts and hands entwine.
An anthem loud, for all to heed,
The power found in every need.

Illuminating the Path

In the twilight's gentle glow,
Step by step, we learn to grow.
With every choice, a light we find,
A journey forged in heart and mind.

The stars above like lanterns shine,
A guide through dark, a path divine.
Through twists and turns, we'll make our way,
With hope as constant, come what may.

Should doubts arise and shadows loom,
We'll hold the light, dispel the gloom.
Together strong, we'll face the night,
For in the dark, we find our light.

With every step, our spirits soar,
Our hearts aligned, we dream of more.
In unity, we walk this road,
With every breath, our courage growed.

The path ahead, though wild and vast,
Each moment lived, a spell is cast.
In every choice, a spark, a flame,
Our souls entwined, we fan the same.

Tapestry of Hope

Threads of gold and shades of blue,
Stitched together, dreams come true.
A tapestry of life we weave,
In every heart, hope to believe.

With every stitch, a story told,
In softest whispers, bold and old.
Colors blend, both dark and bright,
Creating warmth, igniting light.

Through trials faced and battles fought,
In every loss, a lesson taught.
With hands that work and hearts that care,
We build a world, our love to share.

With threads of kindness, courage sewn,
In every clash, a seed is sown.
As love expands, our fabric grows,
A vibrant field, where beauty flows.

So let us weave with threads of grace,
In the tapestry, we find our place.
For hope is bright, a guiding star,
Together, we will travel far.

Horizons of Healing

In the dawn light, hope takes flight,
With whispers of peace, the soul ignites.
Each step forward, the heaviness will fade,
In the embrace of the day, new paths are laid.

Fields of green, where heartbeats sync,
The river flows, a gentle link.
With every heartbeat, we mend and grow,
Toward brighter skies, we let our dreams flow.

Moments of silence, where worries cease,
In the quiet, we find our peace.
Shadows retreat as the light expands,
Together we rise, hand in hand.

A tapestry woven of joy and strife,
Every thread tells the story of life.
With courage, we face the storms that bend,
In horizons of healing, we discover our end.

Transitions in Stillness

Beneath the still sky, time softly flows,
Whispers of change in the hush that grows.
Moments linger, allowing the heart,
To embrace the shifts that gently impart.

In the silence, we listen deep,
Where secrets of growth begin to seep.
Each breath a promise, each sigh a release,
In transitions of stillness, we find our peace.

The dance of the leaves in a soft, warm breeze,
Nature's reminders that change brings ease.
With patience we watch, the world transform,
In quietude, our spirits warm.

Echoes of past lift into the air,
A journey of healing beyond compare.
In the stillness, we gather our strength,
Embracing the journey, we go to great length.

A Dance of Recovery

Step by step, we find our way,
In a dance of recovery, come what may.
With rhythm and grace, we learn to rise,
In the light of new beginnings, we realize.

Every stumble teaches, every fall inspires,
Resilience blossoms, fueled by our fires.
Together we move, in unity's sway,
In the dance of recovery, we seize the day.

With open hearts, we let love lead,
In this journey of healing, we plant the seed.
With laughter and tears, we weave our song,
In each step we take, we'll prove we belong.

The music of life carries us high,
In the embrace of kindness, we learn to fly.
As we sway to the beat of hope's gentle tune,
In the dance of recovery, we reach for the moon.

Broken Pieces into Art

Scattered fragments on the floor,
Once held together, now wanting more.
In shattered dreams, beauty unfolds,
From broken pieces, a masterpiece molds.

With every crack, a story is told,
Of courage and heart, of being bold.
The colors of pain become vibrant hues,
In the canvas of life, we find our muse.

From ruins arise, we gather the light,
In the ashes, we find new sight.
Each piece a treasure, each flaw a part,
In broken pieces, we craft our art.

Embracing imperfections, we choose to create,
From the shards of the past, we shape our fate.
Life's tapestry woven with threads that break,
In broken pieces, the heart can awake.

Tides of Transformation

Waves crash upon the shore,
Whispers of change in their roar.
Each tide brings a new embrace,
Crafting life with gentle grace.

Moonlit paths that guide the way,
Shadows dance where children play.
In the ebb, the flow is found,
Mysteries of the sea abound.

The sands shift beneath our feet,
Life's rhythm a steady beat.
From dawn to dusk, we rise and fall,
Nature's canvas, we heed the call.

Transformations in every hue,
Life renews, and love breaks through.
With each wave, a tale unfolds,
The ocean's secrets, bright and bold.

Through every storm, we learn to swim,
Finding strength when hope seems dim.
In the tides, a lesson clear,
Embrace the change, let go of fear.

Sculpture of Stillness

In quiet realms where shadows play,
Time stands still, night meets the day.
A moment carved in silence deep,
Where secrets of the heart we keep.

The gentle breeze, a soft caress,
Nature breathes in tenderness.
Each leaf whispers tales of rest,
In stillness, we are truly blessed.

In twilight hues, the world unwinds,
A sculptor's touch, the heart aligns.
Within the calm, we find our voice,
In stillness, we rejoice, we choice.

Mountains stand, steadfast and grand,
In their shadows, we understand.
Life's mosaic, piece by piece,
In moments of stillness, we find peace.

Embracing pauses, breaths we take,
In the quiet, new paths we make.
Like frozen art, our souls reflect,
A sculpture of love, we connect.

Canvas of Compassion

Colors blend in tender strokes,
Hearts entwined in silent oaks.
Each brush of kindness paints the sky,
A vibrant world where spirits fly.

The palette rich with every hue,
Gently speaks of me and you.
In every smile and tear we share,
Compassion blooms from heart to care.

In crowded streets or quiet homes,
Every soul, the heart still roams.
We craft a tapestry so wide,
Where love weaves through, a gentle guide.

From darkest nights to brightest days,
The canvas tells of life's great ways.
In kindness wrapped with every thread,
We cherish all the roads we tread.

As artists, we create our fate,
In compassion, we elevate.
Every stroke, a prayer to share,
On this canvas, we declare.

Alchemy of Time

Moments pass like grains of sand,
Fleeting, yet we understand.
With every tick, a chance to grow,
In the heart, the fire we sow.

Time, a river, deep and wide,
Carries dreams on its timeless tide.
In the ebb, we find our ground,
In every memory, love abounds.

Transforming hours to golden light,
In shadows cast, we seek the bright.
With every season, we embrace change,
In the dance of time, we rearrange.

We hold the moments close and dear,
Each laugh, each sigh, each whispered tear.
The alchemy of life we find,
In time's embrace, our souls aligned.

From past to future, paths unfold,
Stories of the brave and bold.
With every heartbeat, we remind,
In the alchemy of time, we're intertwined.

Unraveled and Restitched

Threads of old stories frayed and worn,
Hearts once tethered, now pulled and torn.
In silent hours, we weave anew,
A tapestry bright with shades of you.

With gentle hands, we gather the strands,
Knots of the past, unraveled by plans.
Stitches of hope, both strong and fine,
Mend what was broken, yours and mine.

In the dance of life, we find our way,
Through the fabric of night into the day.
Every piece tells a tale of grace,
Of love that endures time's embrace.

So let us sew with fervor and care,
To stitch together what once was rare.
In the quilt of dreams, we'll find our place,
Unraveled and restitched, a warm embrace.

We stand as one, with colors bright,
In the joy of mending, we unite.
Life's fabric holds, through trials we've faced,
Together we thrive, a bond interlaced.

The Language of Mending

In whispers soft, the heart will speak,
A silent pact when words feel weak.
With gentle touch, we mend the seams,
Building trust from fragile dreams.

With every tear, a lesson learned,
In healing hands, our spirits turned.
Language of love, woven with care,
Every thread a promise we share.

Through storms we weather, through winds we face,
Each stitch a mark of time and space.
In shared embraces, wounds will heal,
The language of mending, a sacred seal.

With courage found in every fray,
Together we rewrite our own way.
In this tapestry of hope we find,
The art of mending, two hearts aligned.

So let us talk in colors bright,
In every shade, we find our light.
The language of mending shall prevail,
In love's embrace, we will not fail.

Solace in the Storm

When thunder roars and shadows loom,
  I seek the quiet within the gloom.
  Raindrops whisper secrets sweet,
  In nature's grasp, my fears retreat.

The wind may howl, but I find peace,
  In chaos where the heart's release.
  For in the storm, I hear the song,
  A symphony where I belong.

Lightning crashes, illuminating skies,
In the tempest's heart, my spirit flies.
Each gust a chance to face the night,
A dance of power, fierce and bright.

With every flash, I learn to trust,
  The magic hidden in the dust.
  Solace found in nature's roar,
  A reminder of what I adore.

So let the storm come, I won't be swayed,
  In tempest's arms, I am not afraid.
  For in this chaos, I shall find,
  The peace that lives within my mind.

The Dawn After Darkness

When night descends and fears take hold,
The heart grows weary, the world feels cold.
But in the hush of twilight's sigh,
A promise lingers, the sun will rise.

In shadows deep, hope finds a way,
To weave through dreams of a brighter day.
Through trials faced, we learn to stand,
With open hearts and steady hands.

The stars will fade with morning's breath,
A whispered grace in life and death.
Each dawn a canvas, fresh and new,
Painting the world in vibrant hue.

So let the darkness come and go,
For in its depths, we learn to grow.
The dawn after darkness brings light's embrace,
A journey onward, a sacred space.

With every sunrise, as shadows flee,
We find our strength, we learn to see.
In each new beginning, life is spun,
The dawn after darkness has just begun.

Wings of Release

In the quiet of the night,
Whispers of freedom take flight.
Carried by dreams on soft air,
Leaving behind all despair.

Feathers of hopes flutter bright,
Chasing the stars, embracing light.
Every burden turned to a breeze,
Soul unshackled, heart at ease.

With every beat, a promise is made,
To rise above, no fear of shade.
Through storms and trials, we will soar,
Finding our path, forevermore.

Beneath the vast and endless sky,
We shed our doubts, learn to fly.
Wings of release, strong and free,
In unity, we find our glee.

Together we dance, nature's song,
In this journey, we all belong.
With every laughter, every sigh,
Wings of release help us to fly.

Echoing Gratitude

In the stillness, whispers resound,
Gratitude's echoes, all around.
Nature's symphony, soft and bright,
Fills our hearts with pure delight.

Each moment that passes, a gift we embrace,
Finding joy in this sacred space.
With open eyes, we start to see,
All the wonders that simply be.

In the laughter of friends and family near,
In the warmth of love, we're free from fear.
Echoing softly, the heartbeats flow,
In every shared memory, affection grows.

Let the world know, there's so much to share,
In the smallest of acts, we show we care.
With each whispered thanks, our spirits rise,
Echoing gratitude fills the skies.

Together we weave a tapestry bright,
Threads of kindness illuminated by light.
Echoing gratitude, a song we sing,
To the beauty of life, our hearts take wing.

Steps Through Shadows

In the twilight, shadows dance,
Silent echoes of a chance.
Each step taken, a journey begun,
Embracing the dark, we reach for the sun.

Through the strife, we learn to grow,
Every challenge helps us glow.
In the labyrinth of fear and doubt,
We find the courage to break out.

The paths we tread, though dimly lit,
Are painted with dreams that perfectly fit.
In the silence, we hear our call,
Steps through shadows lead to it all.

With every heartbeat, a rhythm we find,
Echoing wisdom carefully unlined.
Turning the dark into shades of gold,
With each story, a new truth unfolds.

Together we rise, hand in hand,
Finding light on this promised land.
Through shadows deep, we will persist,
Steps through shadows, a journey of bliss.

Threads of Love

In the tapestry of life, we weave,
Threads of love, we all believe.
With colors bright, our stories intertwine,
Creating bonds that forever shine.

From heart to heart, a gentle touch,
In the small things, we find so much.
Every moment shared, a precious thread,
In the fabric of life, love's spirit is spread.

Through storms we stand, shoulder to shoulder,
With threads of love, we become bolder.
In laughter and in tears, we are one,
In the warmth of connection, battles are won.

With every hug, with every kiss,
Threads of love weave a world of bliss.
In unity's embrace, our hopes grow tall,
Together we rise, we won't let fall.

As seasons change and ages flow,
Threads of love will forever glow.
In this fabric of life, we'll find our place,
Threads of love, a tapestry of grace.

Seeds of Strength

In the soil, dreams take root,
Nurtured by rain, and light so sweet.
Tiny sprouts reach for the sky,
With every gust, they learn to fly.

Against the storm, they bend and sway,
Finding courage in the fray.
Each leaf a testament to the fight,
Growing deeper, reaching height.

In silence, strength begins to bloom,
Quiet whispers chase away the gloom.
From humble seeds, bold flowers rise,
Painting colors across the skies.

With patience, they weather the past,
Building a future, strong and vast.
In unity, they stand so tall,
Together, they can conquer all.

Hope is planted, and so it grows,
Through every struggle, beauty shows.
In gardens where resilience thrives,
The seeds of strength are what survives.

Fusion of Fragments

Scattered pieces find their way,
Mended hearts begin to play.
In misaligned shapes, a spark ignites,
Creating magic in the nights.

The stories shared, both old and new,
In every crack, a glimmer shines through.
With every blend, a unique song,
Celebrating where we all belong.

Each fragment tells a tale untold,
In the warmth, the colors unfold.
Together, we weave a vibrant cloth,
In the tapestry, we find what's lost.

Embracing chaos, we intertwine,
In every crease, our spirits align.
This fusion born from pain and grace,
Emerges resilient, time can't erase.

In unity, we rise and thrive,
From shattered dreams, we come alive.
A mosaic built on trust's embrace,
In this kaleidoscope, we find our place.

Navigating the Shadows

In the twilight, whispers blend,
Footsteps falter, yet we mend.
Through the haze, we search for light,
Chasing visions in the night.

Shadows dance, secrets unfold,
Guiding dreams both brave and bold.
A flicker sparks within the dark,
Illuminating each lost mark.

With courage stitched to every seam,
We unravel the weight of the dream.
As stars align in the midnight blue,
We learn the path to push on through.

In the stillness, strength is found,
With every heartbeat, we are bound.
Navigating through what we fear,
Finding solace in each tear.

So here we stand, hand in hand,
Lost souls thriving, a vibrant band.
In shadows deep, we find our thread,
Together forging paths ahead.

Heartbeats of Change

In quiet moments, echoes ring,
The pulse of life begins to sing.
A shift occurs in the gentle breeze,
Carrying whispers of what will be.

Awakening hearts, a newfound beat,
In the distance, hope feels sweet.
With every change, we learn and grow,
Through the tides that ebb and flow.

In unison, we rise and fall,
Each heartbeat answers nature's call.
Together, we forge a new design,
Crafting futures, intertwining lines.

Charting paths through shifting sands,
With open hearts, we take our stands.
In every breath, we feel the flight,
Beneath the stars, we share the night.

So listen close, let yearning lead,
In the rhythm, plant each seed.
For heartbeats pulse with love and grace,
Embracing change, we find our place.

The Symphony of Healing

In stillness, hearts begin to mend,
Notes of grace softly blend.
Whispers of time help us to see,
The power of love sets us free.

Through shadows, light will always shine,
A gentle touch, two souls entwine.
Melodies of hope fill the air,
In harmony, we rise and dare.

The beats of kindness, strong yet sweet,
In every rhythm, we find our feet.
Music flows like a river wide,
Together, we'll take the healing ride.

From silence, we craft our song,
Creating a bond that feels so strong.
In every note, the past we face,
We find ourselves in healing's grace.

With every chord, old pain will fade,
A symphony of love is made.
In unity, our voices soar,
A healing choir forever more.

Blossoms from Ashes

From embers faint, new life will rise,
A testament beneath the skies.
Petals soft, yet strong and bold,
In warmth of sun, stories unfold.

Once barren ground, now vibrant hue,
Dreams emerge, refreshed and new.
Amidst the ruins, beauty thrives,
Hope ignites, and passion dives.

Each blossom tells of trials past,
Resilience grows, its roots are vast.
In every shade, a tale to tell,
Of soaring high and falling well.

Beneath the storm, we found our way,
With courage bright, we face the day.
The ashes speak of love once lost,
Now seeds of joy, worth any cost.

Through fire and pain, our spirits soar,
Embracing life forevermore.
From ashes, we find our true release,
In nature's cradle, there is peace.

Reflections on Reconciliation

In mirrored hearts, we find our way,
Past shadows fade, they drift away.
Honesty blooms in tender light,
Where love can thrive, dispelling fright.

To bridge the chasm born of pride,
With open arms, we reach and guide.
Words once spoken find a new tone,
Forgiveness whispers, we're not alone.

Every tear shared washes pain clean,
In every story, a love serene.
We turn the page, the past behind,
In unity's grace, our hearts aligned.

With patience woven through our thread,
Compassion grows where once we bled.
Together, we face the storms ahead,
In whispers sweet, our fears are shed.

Reflections deep in the still night,
We hold our truths and embrace the light.
Two souls, a journey, now intertwined,
In reconciliation, peace we find.

Nature's Embrace

In forest deep, where shadows play,
Nature wraps us, come what may.
With every breeze that dances near,
Whispers of earth, we long to hear.

Beneath the stars, our worries cease,
The moon's soft glow brings gentle peace.
Each rustling leaf tells tales of time,
In nature's arms, we find our rhyme.

A river flows, its secrets kept,
Through valleys wide where dreams are wept.
With every wave that crashes down,
We feel the pulse of life's own crown.

Mountains high, a silent guide,
In their embrace, we learn to glide.
The sun will rise, bringing light anew,
In nature's love, our spirits grew.

Through seasons change, we dance along,
In every heartbeat, nature's song.
Together, we become whole once more,
In nature's embrace, our spirits soar.

Echoes of Serenity

In the hush of dawn's embrace,
Whispers dance, the softest grace.
Leaves flutter down like gentle sighs,
Nature's peace beneath the skies.

Rippling streams in quiet flow,
Mirrored skies, a tranquil glow.
Every breath a chance to feel,
Harmony that seems so real.

Mountains stand, timeless and grand,
Cradling dreams in their strong hands.
Misty mornings, a calming breath,
Life unfolds, a sweet caress.

Stars will twinkle in the night,
Guiding hearts with silver light.
In these moments, still and free,
We find solace, you and me.

The echoes linger, soft and clear,
Reminding us why we are here.
In every shadow, in every hue,
Serenity whispers, ever true.

Patchwork of the Soul

Threads of color weave and blend,
Stories that our hearts transcend.
Every stitch a tale to tell,
Sewn with love, where shadows dwell.

In laughter's light, in sorrow's shade,
Memories of joy will never fade.
Pieces held by hands of time,
Creating art, a life sublime.

Faded photographs, whispers bright,
Moments captured in soft light.
Each fragment tells of where we've been,
A tapestry of what lies within.

With every patch, we learn, we grow,
In the stitches, our spirits flow.
Hearts united, a vibrant whole,
This beautiful patchwork of the soul.

Life's design, both rough and smooth,
In every scar, a mark to soothe.
Together we create the view,
Patterns made for me and you.

Fragments of Light

In the cracks of the darkest night,
A spark ignites, a flickering light.
Hope emerges, gentle and bright,
Guiding the lost toward what is right.

Shattered dreams, in pieces laid,
Yet beauty grows in the light's cascade.
Each fragment shines with a story told,
Woven whispers in silver and gold.

Sunrise paints the world anew,
Casting colors, a vibrant hue.
From tiny seeds of faith, we start,
Gathering strength from the light in the heart.

Even in shadows, glimmers gleam,
Fragments of light become a dream.
With open eyes, we start to see,
The brilliance that sets our spirits free.

So let the light guide every way,
In fragments found, we choose to stay.
Together we shine through the night,
Embracing the dance of pure delight.

Seasons of the Heart

Spring arrives with blooms so bright,
Awakening love, pure delight.
Soft petals burst with every sigh,
In the warmth, our spirits fly.

Summer days with golden rays,
Laughter echoes in sunlit ways.
Moments linger, sweet and bold,
Stories of warmth, forever told.

Autumn whispers with a gentle breeze,
Leaves cascade like memories.
A tapestry of crimson and gold,
In our hearts, the stories unfold.

Winter's chill, a quiet retreat,
Fireside dreams in soft heartbeat.
Wrapped in love, we find our way,
In stillness, our souls gently sway.

Each season brings its own embrace,
A journey through time, a sacred space.
With open hearts, we heed the call,
Seasons of love, a gift to all.

Dance of the Inner Light

In the quiet of the dawn,
Shadows begin to sway,
Colors whisper and spin,
Chasing the night away.

Hearts rise like the sun,
Casting warmth to the ground,
Footsteps find their rhythm,
In the space where hope is found.

Winds carry gentle tunes,
Harmonies soft and sweet,
Every beat like a drum,
Echoing in the street.

Fingers reach for the stars,
Grasping dreams of old,
In this dance of the spirit,
New stories unfold.

With each twirl and leap,
We break free from despair,
The inner light will guide,
As we dance through the air.

Seeds of Self-Discovery

In the soil of our hearts,
Lies a potential vast,
Nurtured by hopes and dreams,
Waiting to bloom at last.

Whispers of the soul call,
Beneath the surface clear,
With every choice we make,
New paths will soon appear.

Tides of change wash o'er us,
Cleansing doubts from the past,
Planting seeds of knowledge,
In the shadows cast.

Awakening the truth,
That's hidden deep inside,
With gentle hands we dig,
In this journey, we bide.

From tiny sprouts of thought,
Great forests will arise,
As we tend to our spirits,
And reach for the skies.

Whispers of Renewal

In the stillness of the night,
Stars begin to glow,
Speaking tales of the past,
In a soft, gentle flow.

The moon casts silver beams,
Across the silent lake,
Each ripple holds a secret,
Of dawn yet to awake.

Breath of the wind carries,
Memories lost in time,
Reaching for the fragments,
In a melody sublime.

Every moment a chance,
To shed what once was known,
In the dance of rebirth,
A new seed shall be sown.

So let whispers of renewal,
Guide us on our way,
For within each ending,
Lives the start of a new day.

Beneath the Surface of Scars

Beneath the surface of scars,
Lies a story untold,
Wounds that have shaped us,
In whispers of bold.

Each mark tells a tale,
Of battles we've faced,
The courage to rise,
In a life interlaced.

Moments of darkness,
Turn to wisdom and light,
As we glean from our trials,
Emerging from the night.

There's beauty in healing,
In the lessons we find,
Resilience and strength,
Are intertwined.

So let us embrace,
The art of our scars,
For beneath these stories,
Shine our true avatars.

Threads of Serenity

In the stillness of the night,
Whispers dance on silver light.
Each breath a soft embrace,
Calmness settles in this space.

Stars above begin to glow,
Guiding dreams where rivers flow.
Ties of peace, a gentle thread,
Woven thoughts that softly spread.

Leaves are rustling in the breeze,
Nature's lullabies at ease.
Every moment, pure and bright,
Cradles us in endless light.

The world fades into a hush,
Where dreams weave and worries crush.
In the fabric of the night,
Threads of love hold us so tight.

Awake we find a gentle morn,
With new hopes and hearts reborn.
Threads of life entwined in grace,
Serenity's warm embrace.

Corals of the Soul

Beneath the waves where colors blend,
Lies a world where dreams extend.
Corals dance in oceans deep,
Secrets of the heart they keep.

Every hue, a story shines,
In the depths, the spirit aligns.
A sanctuary of pure desire,
Igniting the soul's inner fire.

Echoes of the tides arise,
Whispers like ancient lullabies.
In the currents, we find our way,
Guided by the light of day.

With every pulse, the ocean sways,
Carrying hopes where laughter plays.
Through the depths, let courage grow,
In the sea, our spirits flow.

Awash in beauty, hearts set free,
Dancing in the symphony.
Corals sing, our souls entwined,
In the depths, true peace we find.

The Heart's Mosaic

Fragments of life painted bright,
Pieced together in the night.
Every shard a sacred tale,
Woven together, we prevail.

Colors clash yet complement,
In the chaos, time is spent.
Building blocks of love and pain,
Crafting beauty from the rain.

Layers deep, emotions flow,
In this art, we come to know.
Every heart holds a place,
In the mosaic, endless grace.

Unified through every scar,
Finding light in who we are.
With every heartbeat, life unfolds,
A masterpiece in vibrant golds.

Voices echo, stories blend,
Mosaic hearts that never end.
In the tapestry we see,
The beauty of you and me.

Breaths of Bravery

In shadows deep, we find our might,
Facing fears that cloud the light.
With each breath, a step is made,
In the heart, the courage laid.

Mountains rise, the path is steep,
Yet within, the heart won't sleep.
Chasing dreams with open eyes,
In the struggle, we arise.

Voices whisper, doubts may grow,
But within, a fire aglow.
Every heartbeat, strong and true,
Propels us on to what is new.

Through the storms, we learn to stand,
Side by side, we join our hand.
Breaths of hope fill up the sky,
With every leap, we learn to fly.

Unwritten tales that carve the way,
Shining bright with every day.
Though the journey may be long,
Together, we will rise, be strong.

When the Soul Sings

In the quiet, a note does rise,
Whispers of dreams 'neath endless skies.
Hearts entwined in gentle grace,
Melodies dance in a sacred place.

With every beat, the world stands still,
Echoes of joy, an unseen thrill.
Life's rhythm flows through tender hands,
Together we weave, as fate commands.

Stars awaken in the night,
Songs of love bring pure delight.
A harmony known deep within,
When the soul sings, we all begin.

Voices rise like morning dew,
Shimmering hopes in shades of blue.
With each refrain, hearts lift and soar,
When the soul sings, we want for more.

Join the chorus, feel the light,
In every shadow, hope takes flight.
For passion reigns where dreams ignite,
When the soul sings, darkness takes flight.

The Bridge from Grief

In silence deep, a heart will mourn,
Lost in echoes, a soul is torn.
Yet in the night, a flicker glows,
A bridge of hope, through pain it flows.

Tears may fall like gentle rain,
Each drop whispers of love and pain.
With every sigh, the heart will heal,
From ashes rise, the spirit feels.

In shared memories, we find our way,
A path to light from shades of gray.
Hold the moments, let them breathe,
In grief, we learn to hope, believe.

Time will weave a softer thread,
With every loss, new love is bred.
Across the bridge, we'll find our grace,
In the sorrow, a warm embrace.

So take my hand, let's walk anew,
Through valleys dark, to skies so blue.
From grief we build a story bright,
A bridge of love, our guiding light.

Awakening the Spirit

In the dawn's embrace, dreams unfold,
Whispers of wisdom, tales retold.
Awakening light in every heart,
A journey begins, a brand new start.

Beneath the stars, our spirits soar,
Seeking treasures on distant shores.
With open arms, the world we greet,
In every pulse, the rhythm's beat.

Nature sings in vibrant hues,
Guiding footsteps, old paths renew.
With every breath, let courage flow,
Awakening strength, we rise and grow.

Through trials faced, we learn to fly,
Releasing fears that held us high.
In the embrace of each new day,
Awakening spirit finds its way.

So let us dance with hearts aglow,
In the light of love, we'll bravely go.
With each sunrise, a soul reborn,
Awakening dreams, a new dawn sworn.

Unseen Beauty

Amidst the noise, a whisper calls,
Hidden treasures behind the walls.
In quiet moments, stillness grows,
Unseen beauty, the heart bestows.

The softest touch, a gentle sigh,
In every glance, beneath the sky.
Life's little wonders, often missed,
Unseen beauty, wrapped in bliss.

Like petals kissed by morning dew,
A silent grace that feels so true.
In laughter shared, in tears we find,
Unseen beauty, a thread entwined.

Through every struggle, every fight,
A spark of hope ignites the night.
In simple things, our hearts align,
Unseen beauty, forever shine.

So take the time, let moments flow,
In stillness breathe, let kindness grow.
For in each heartbeat, truth we see,
Unseen beauty sets us free.

Transformation of the Spirit

In the quiet dawn of a new day,
Hope whispers softly, lighting the way.
Hearts awaken, shedding the night,
Strength grows deeper, embracing the light.

From the ashes, we rise and ascend,
Our burdens release, new paths to trend.
Wings unfurl, ready to soar,
With every heartbeat, we dream more.

Lessons learned in the shadows past,
Carved in wisdom, meant to last.
We transform, bloom fierce and bright,
Our spirits dance in pure delight.

Boundless courage fuels the fire,
We break the chains, rise ever higher.
With love as the compass, we journey wide,
In the transformation of the spirit, we confide.

Together we weave a tapestry bright,
Strings of hope, love, and insight.
Hand in hand, we embrace the call,
In the dance of life, we'll never fall.

Echoing Silence

In the stillness, whispers arise,
Echoing softly, beneath the skies.
Voices of dreams, spaced far apart,
Sown in the silence, a tender heart.

Shadows linger, where fears abide,
Yet in the quiet, truth cannot hide.
A gentle murmur flows, pure and clear,
Inviting the soul to draw near.

Each thought a ripple, soft and profound,
In echoing silence, a peace is found.
Listen closely, let the stillness speak,
In calm embrace, we gather the meek.

With every heartbeat, we learn to trust,
In moments of silence, the spirit must.
Barefoot on whispers of hope so bright,
We dance with the echoes, lost in the night.

In this stillness, let the heart mend,
Find solace in silence, our stoutest friend.
With open hearts, we breathe in grace,
In the echoing silence, we find our place.

The Blossoming Spirit

A bud in the morning, kissed by the dew,
Emerging with colors, vibrant and true.
Petals unfurling, reaching for skies,
In the dance of the sun, our spirit will rise.

Roots deep in the earth, drawing life's lore,
Echoes of wisdom we long to explore.
In rich, fertile soil, dreams take their form,
As the spirit blooms, embracing the warm.

Every flower tells tales of the past,
Of struggles and triumphs, shadows cast.
In a garden of dreams, we find what's real,
The blossoming spirit learns how to feel.

Colors intertwine in a magical blend,
Every moment, a journey, a bend.
Together we flourish, a tapestry bright,
In the flowering fields, we find our light.

Let the fragrance of hope fill the air,
In the garden of hearts, we tenderly share.
With every blossom, the spirit is free,
In the dance of the wind, we find harmony.

Chasing Light through Shadows

In the twilight's embrace, shadows unfold,
A whisper of stories, both timid and bold.
Chasing the light that flickers and sways,
Guiding our journey through night's winding maze.

Each shadow conceals a flicker of grace,
A lesson in patience, a moment in space.
As darkness surrounds, we search for the gleam,
In the dance of the shadows, we nurture the dream.

Hope becomes lantern, shining our way,
Illuminating paths where the lost go astray.
With hearts ignited, we follow the spark,
In the chase for the light, we conquer the dark.

Through echoes of silence, we wander and roam,
In the shadows, we forge our new home.
As light beckons softly, we dare to believe,
That within every shadow, the heart learns to weave.

Together we rise, united in flight,
Chasing the dreams that emerge from the night.
In the tapestry woven of shadow and gleam,
We find our strength in the light of the dream.

Healing Tides

Waves crash softly on the shore,
Whispers of pain start to soar.
Each splash a promise to begin,
To cleanse the heart and let love in.

With every tide, a change unfolds,
A dance of courage, stories told.
The ocean's rhythm, a soothing balm,
Restores the spirit, brings a calm.

Shells and stones, treasures aligned,
Nature's gifts, beauty designed.
Embrace the ebb, embrace the flow,
In healing tides, we learn to grow.

Stars above twinkle in grace,
Guiding souls to find their place.
The night whispers secrets untold,
In the waves, our stories unfold.

From stormy seas to tranquil skies,
Hope emerges, and spirit flies.
The journey's long, but worth each stride,
For in the waves, we learn to ride.

Moments of Rebirth

In quiet hours, a seed takes root,
From darkness, it stirs, begins to shoot.
Sunlight breaks through, a gentle kiss,
A moment of rebirth, pure bliss.

Each day dawns with chance anew,
To shed the past and embrace the view.
With whispered hopes, we reach for the sky,
In moments of change, we learn to fly.

A butterfly breaks from its shell,
Transforming pain into a spell.
What once was lost, now finds its way,
In moments of rebirth, we sway.

As rain nourishes the thirsty ground,
New life emerges, beauty found.
Through trials endured, we come alive,
In moments of rebirth, we thrive.

Let every heartbeat sing a song,
For in rebirth, we all belong.
With open hearts, let the journey start,
In moments of rebirth, we find our heart.

Journey to Wholeness

Step by step, the path unfolds,
With courage born from stories told.
Every stumble leads to grace,
In the journey, we find our place.

Mountains high and valleys low,
A dance of shadows, a vibrant glow.
Through trials faced, our spirits soar,
In the journey, we seek for more.

Each breath a chance to start anew,
To weave the past with shades of blue.
In every tear, a seed of light,
In the journey, we embrace the night.

Moments linger, memories bind,
In every heart, a truth we find.
As pieces align, a tapestry grows,
In the journey, our true self shows.

With every step, we shed the guise,
In authenticity, the spirit flies.
The canvas of life, rich and bold,
In the journey, we find our gold.

Quietude

In stillness lies a world profound,
Whispers of peace, a sacred sound.
Softly falling, like autumn leaves,
In quietude, the spirit breathes.

The heart finds rhythm, steady and slow,
In gentle moments, we learn to grow.
Silence wraps us in a warm embrace,
In quietude, we find our space.

The mind unwinds, like vines that creep,
Into the corners where secrets sleep.
Each thought a ripple, calm and light,
In quietude, we find our sight.

With nature's breath, time ebbs away,
A moment cherished, a soft bouquet.
In every silence, a voice unique,
In quietude, the heart can speak.

Let the world spin in its haste,
For in the still, we find our grace.
In every heartbeat, a gentle cue,
In quietude, we start anew.

Courage

In the face of fear, we stand our ground,
With whispers of strength in every sound.
Each heartbeat, a call to rise,
In courage, we see the skies.

Facing storms with heads held high,
In the darkest moments, we learn to fly.
With every step, the shadows fade,
In courage, our truth is laid.

From ashes of doubt, new flames ignite,
A fierce resolve, a shining light.
In every challenge, a chance to shine,
In courage, the stars align.

Brave souls gather, their stories shared,
Weaving strength where once was scared.
With open hearts, we journey forth,
In courage, we find our worth.

Let the winds howl and the waves crash,
For in courage, our spirits clash.
Together we rise, hand in hand,
In courage, united we stand.

Kaleidoscope of Hope

In dreams we find the light,
Colors dancing, hearts take flight.
Each moment holds a spark,
Guiding us through the dark.

Waves of laughter, shades of grace,
Every corner, a warm embrace.
In this tapestry so wide,
Hope's bright threads are woven inside.

Whispers soft like morning dew,
Painting skies in radiant hue.
With every step, we redefine,
The beauty of this grand design.

Through shadows, we will tread,
Chasing dreams, where angels tread.
In unity, our spirits gleam,
Held together in this dream.

With open hearts, we rise above,
Creating worlds with peace and love.
In the kaleidoscope we see,
Hope unfurls, wild and free.

Shattered Whispers

In silence, secrets drift away,
Torn apart, in disarray.
Fragments of a whispered sigh,
Echoes of a once bright sky.

Every glance holds a story dear,
Fleeting moments, mixed with fear.
Lost in thoughts of what once was,
Faded dreams, a silent buzz.

Mirrors crack with truths untold,
Shattered echoes, growing bold.
Yet in the shards, a glimmer stays,
A hope that fights through the haze.

In midnight's breath, we take a stand,
Rebuilding worlds with trembling hands.
Through the pain, a lesson learned,
In shattered whispers, hearts have burned.

From the rubble, we will rise,
Finding strength in tear-streaked eyes.
For in each fracture, light will glow,
Guiding us where love can grow.

Soaring Above the Storm

In winds that howl and skies that cry,
We spread our wings and learn to fly.
Over mountains, through the rain,
Finding freedom through the pain.

Clouds may gather, shadows fall,
Yet courage whispers through it all.
With hearts like eagles, fierce and bold,
We chase horizons made of gold.

Riding currents, wild and free,
Breaking chains and setting free.
Above the storms that want to bind,
We find the strength to seek and find.

So let the thunder shake the land,
We'll rise above, hand in hand.
For every tempest must subside,
In hope and love, we will abide.

With every challenge that we face,
We find our wings, our rightful place.
Soaring high, through darkest night,
Together, we embrace the light.

Reverberations of the Heart

In quiet moments, souls connect,
Every heartbeat, deep respect.
Whispers linger in the air,
Echoing love beyond compare.

Through the laughter and the tears,
We find solace through the years.
In every glance, a promise made,
In every step, our fears allayed.

Threads of hope, they intertwine,
Creating bonds, pure and divine.
Every pulse, a timeless song,
In this rhythm, we belong.

With open arms, we stand as one,
Facing battles, rising sun.
In the symphony of our lives,
Each note a truth, where love survives.

So let the echoes fill the air,
Reverberate with love and care.
In harmony, our hearts will beat,
In every moment, love's heartbeat.

The Journey Inwards

In silence deep, I start my quest,
To find the heart, to know the rest.
With whispers soft, the shadows blend,
A dance of thoughts that never end.

A mirror shows what feels so right,
While secrets hide beyond the light.
With every step, I learn to see,
The soul within, so wild and free.

Through valleys low and mountains high,
I trace the paths where echoes lie.
Each step unveils a hidden truth,
The wisdom wrapped in fleeting youth.

The journey winds, it bends, it breaks,
In every choice, a lesson takes.
With courage held and fear embraced,
I find my way, my truth is faced.

As shadows fade, I feel the glow,
Of all the love I've come to know.
With open heart, I take a breath,
And cherish life, defying death.

Tides of Forgiveness

The ocean waves roll in and out,
As whispered words dispel all doubt.
Forgiveness flows like ebbing tide,
Embracing pain we used to hide.

Each grain of sand tells a tale,
Of struggles fought, of dreams that pale.
Yet through the storm, a light appears,
To wash away our darkest fears.

We learn to let the past unfurl,
As seashells dance and waves all swirl.
With open hearts, we dare to mend,
And find that love can be our friend.

Embracing change, we start anew,
As tide and time create a view.
With every wave that softly brushes,
We find the strength that gently crushes.

Let go of anger, set it free,
And watch as hearts unite with glee.
In seas of hope, we find our way,
On tides of grace, we choose to stay.

Crafting Tomorrow

With hands of hope, we shape the clay,
Molding dreams that light the way.
Each thought, a spark that starts to grow,
A vision born, a seed we sow.

The future waits with open arms,
Inviting us to weave new charms.
With every choice, we set the pace,
And step into a brighter space.

Through struggles faced and lessons learned,
We build a bridge, the tides have turned.
With every breath, we paint the sky,
And let our hopes begin to fly.

In courage found, we march ahead,
With every word, a truth we spread.
For in the work, our hearts align,
And craft a future, bold and fine.

The canvas stretches wide and free,
Each stroke of passion, chance to be.
With vision clear, we claim our role,
In crafting tomorrow, we find our soul.

The Light After the Rain

When clouds roll in and shadows fall,
The world feels small, the pain a call.
Yet through the storm, a promise gleams,
A hope renewed, a tapestry of dreams.

Each drop that falls holds lessons true,
As petals dance with every hue.
The earth awakens, fresh and bright,
And whispers tales of pure delight.

With every thunder, hearts may quake,
Yet from the ashes, we shall wake.
For every tear that finds its place,
Will bloom anew with tender grace.

The sun peeks out, the rainbow bends,
As nature's art begins to blend.
With light like gold, the world transforms,
As hope rises and love conforms.

Embrace the joy that follows strife,
For after rain comes vibrant life.
In every storm, the light will reign,
And guide us home, fresh from the rain.